Bible Study That Works

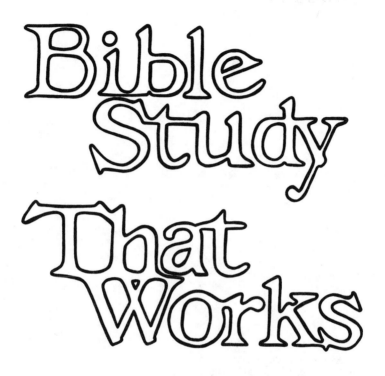

Bible Study That Works

DAVID L. THOMPSON

FRANCIS ASBURY PRESS
of Zondervan Publishing House

Grand Rapids, Michigan

095179

BIBLE STUDY THAT WORKS
Copyright © 1982 by David L. Thompson

FRANCIS ASBURY PRESS is an imprint of Zondervan
Publishing House, 1415 Lake Drive, S.E.,
Grand Rapids, Michigan 49506

First Zondervan printing 1984

Printed in the United States of America

84 85 86 87 88 89 90 / 10 9 8 7 6 5 4 3 2 1

To my
Mother and Father
at whose knees I first learned
to love and live God's Word

FOREWORD

David Thompson has given the Bible reader a challenge—to do something even better than reading. It is a challenge to really *study* the Word of God. Not only does he exhort but he also instructs. In plain language and with practical applications the reader is led into creative procedures which make Bible study so exciting and fulfilling.

Based upon the premise that sequence is important, he emphasizes that observation should precede interpretation and application to one's life and time should conclude the search. Wisely he explains how best to use and not misuse the innumerable "helps" to Bible study.

Among the many helpful features of the volume is the author's perspective of Bible versions; another is the emphasis on context as well as text. The listing of different steps for fruitful study is fundamental. The reader who follows this guide into creative study will be richly rewarded.

George Allen Turner
Professor Emeritus of English Bible
Asbury Theological Seminary

PREFACE

Lay people and clergy alike exhibit a growing appetite for serious study of the Bible. This groundswell of interest in the direct study of the Bible has, in recent years, called forth a number of popular presentations of inductive Bible study to lead non-specialists beyond superficial reading of the Word of God.

Like several of the other popular works on Bible study method, *Bible Study That Works* owes an obvious debt at innumerable points to the writing and teaching of Dr. Robert A. Traina, Professor of English Bible at Asbury Theological Seminary and current dean of inductive Bible study in the vernacular in North America. Dr. Traina's excellent work, *Methodical Bible Study*, cited for further study in each chapter here, has influenced both the content and outline of this work in obvious ways.

I must also state my profound debt to Dr. George Allen Turner. In the fall of 1962, in his course on the Gospel of John at Asbury Theological Seminary, he captured me for the sort of Bible study described in this work. To both Dr. Traina and Dr. Turner, my beloved teachers and esteemed colleagues, I gladly acknowledge my debt and express my joy in their continuing inspiration and instruction in my study of the Scripture.

This modest contribution to the ministry of presenting sound Bible study method in non-technical language grew out of a series of articles which appeared in *The Wesleyan Advocate* in 1977. It is my happy privilege to express my appreciation to Dr. George E. Failing, editor of *The Wesleyan Advocate*, both for his cooperation in the use of those articles which appear here in revised and expanded form, and also for the example of his own clear-minded study of the Scriptures.

David L. Thompson, Wilmore, Kentucky

TABLE OF CONTENTS

Bible Study That Works

CHAPTER I

BIBLE STUDY: THE WHAT AND
WHY OF IT, AND MORE

Three questions demand an answer before any hints on Bible study can be considered. First, *"What is* Bible study?" Second, *"Why study* the Bible?" and third, *"What Bible* should I study?"

WHAT IS BIBLE STUDY?

To answer the first question, Bible study is *study*, and it is study of the *Bible.* Bible study is not Bible memorization or Bible reading alone. It is not casual acquaintance with the Bible, nor even frequent use of the Bible. Neither is Bible study carrying, quoting, believing, or defending the Bible. Surprisingly enough, it is not even a line by line comment or a verse by verse "sharing" on the Bible, whether done by the pastor, by a group, or by a solitary saint.

Bible study is the regular, careful, systematic *examination* of the Word of God, with an alert mind and a prayerful, open heart. Worthwhile Bible study requires effort. But it is well within the reach of any person of average intelligence.

Furthermore, Bible study is the study of *the Bible.* That would appear self-evident. But a survey of the numerous "Bible study" booklets purchased avidly by contemporary Christians of varying persuasions quickly shows the opposite. In spite of all the effort and good intentions currently focused on "Bible study," the amount of actual study of the Bible being done is surprisingly small. Too many "Bible study" booklets engage the student in one- or two-word, question and answer exercises. They never do lead to a comprehension of the biblical books or passages as units, penned to real people at specific times to meet specific needs. They do not foster a grasp of the great biblical themes and their profound, practical implications for twentieth century life.

That is, of course, not to gainsay a sincere approach to God's Word by whatever means. It is to point out that very few Bible study "helps" currently available lead students to more than a superficial grasp of the Bible. Even fewer give sincere seekers methods by which they can independently and intelligently probe the Word *for themselves!*

Incidentally, it is well to remember that the study of a devotional book and the reading of Christian literature (even commentaries and Bible dictionaries!), though certainly recommended, are simply not Bible study, for which there is no substitute in Christian growth. Bible study is the study of the Bible!

WHY STUDY THE BIBLE?

The second question must be answered: *"Why* study
the Bible?" Obviously because of its place as the greatest
book in world literature, because of its formidable influence on the history and literature of the world, East and
West, one must study the Bible if he or she would be
an educated person.

But, more important for every Christian, one must
study the Bible because of the crucial role of God's Word
in evangelism and Christian nurture. The Word of God is
the Holy Spirit's primary tool for renovation of character
and development of Christian conscience. Contrary to
the notion perpetuated by some preaching and much
testimony, permanent, life directing character change does
not come by some mystical, irresistible sweep of God's
Spirit through our being. Rather, as Jesus and the apostles
clearly taught, we are changed within as *we learn* God's
will by His Word, and *we choose* it as our way by His
grace and Spirit. "Sanctify them by the truth," said Jesus.
"Thy *Word* is truth" (John 17.17; compare also Ephesians
4.20-23; Colossians 3.9-10).

If one would "walk as Jesus walked" (I John 2.6),
how will one know, as a matter of fact, how Jesus did walk
among people? How did He treat women? What was His
attitude toward religious tradition? What did He think was
important in worship? What principles governed His
actions? There is only one place where a sure and enduring answer is to be found—the Bible! If we would be like
Jesus we must learn His way through the Word and then
by His grace choose it daily.

Closely related is the Bible's role in developing Christian conscience. One might think that, having given one's life to Christ, the Christian would almost intuitively know right from wrong in the world. But it is not so. On the contrary, if there is anything stressed by the apostle Paul, it is that the things often judged to be signs of piety and deep spirituality by good people, are precisely the litter with which the path *away* from faith and grace is strewn (see especially Galatians 3, Colossians 2, and Romans 14). God's idea of right is disclosed in the person of Jesus and the way of faith in Him. This idea of right, "God's right way" (Romans 3.21), must instruct our conscience. The textbook again is the Bible.

For this reason, the *first* step in Bible study for the Christian is really *prayer*—prayer that the same Spirit who inspired the writers of God's Word may inspire and illuminate our minds as we study, prayer for a humble and teachable mind. Although it will not often be mentioned hereafter, this first step in Bible study is the context in which all the rest of it takes place.

Why study the Bible—independently, regularly, directly? If I would know Christ's way and grow in it, there is little choice!

DOES GOD USE "THEES" AND "THOUS"?

"What Bible should I study?" Discussion of Bible study method always raises this question. First, study a Bible *in your own dialect*. The whole point of the Bible is communication. Unless you regularly communicate in fourteenth to seventeenth or eighteenth century English, seriously question advice to *restrict* your Bible study to any of the pre-nineteenth century versions. Rather, one should use several versions, including respected older ones, but also encompassing good translations in modern English closest to the language you use.

Second, use one of the standard, non-paraphrasing versions as a *basis* for careful study. Then, for increased insight compare this basic study text with several others new and old, paraphrasing and not. It is rarely a question here of choosing between "good" and "bad" translations. It is rather a matter of selecting a text appropriate to the use you intend. The *King James Version* (KJV), the *New King James Version* (NKJV), the *American Standard Version* (ASV), the *New American Standard Version* (NASV), and the *Revised Standard Version* (RSV) are all examples of standard texts and for careful study are preferable to the more paraphrasing ones.

Paraphrased, expanded renderings are excellent for rapid reading, for general survey, or for use as a commentary of sorts. But they are not suitable for detailed study. The *Living Bible, Today's English Version* (TEV or *Good News*), and Phillips' translations are among the most popular modern paraphrases. The *New International Version* (NIV) and the *New English Bible* (NEB) stand somewhere in between these two groups of texts as far as their freedom in translation is concerned. All translations are interpretive to some degree; none can or should be completely literal.

A review of Romans 8.9 in several translations illustrates the inadvisability of making a paraphrase or a non-standard translation the *basis* of your careful study. Here the NIV reads, "You, however, are *controlled* not by

15

your sinful nature but by the Spirit. . . ." The *Living Bible* is similar. These renderings are fine *unless* one is interested in the specific question as to wherher or not one is actually controlled by either a "lower nature" or by the Holy Spirit. Here the more interpretive treatment will give a premature answer, if not an incorrect one. For contrary to what one often hears, the fruit of the Spirit is *not Spirit-control*, but *self-control* under the *leadership* of the Spirit. (Cf. Romans 8:12-14 and Galatians 5.23, KJV or RSV.) Any of the standard versions gives here a more neutral, less interpretive translation, ". . . in the flesh/Spirit," which leaves the question open for students of the Scriptures themselves to decide. (A related difficulty appears in the TEV, Galatians 5.25.)

Parenthetically, one must raise a caution with regard to the whole matter of the use of numerous English versions (plural!). Although diligent Bible students will consult several renderings of the texts they examine carefully, they *should* decide which standard version will be their base for study and make it their point of reference. They should memorize it, quote it, pass it on to their family and friends, make it part of their very being. Only in this way can one overcome the most ironic hazard of the ready availability of numerous English versions, the tendency to read them all and *memorize none.*

1. But *why* should you study the Bible in your own dialect as opposed to older forms of English? There are three compelling reasons. First, study in your dialect *to take seriously the pattern of biblical revelation itself—God's commitment to communicate.* God spoke to people in varying cultures and in succeeding centuries in the language of *their own day*, not in previously canonized,

16

"sacred languages." Linguistic developments within the Bible itself readily attest to this fact. The period from Abraham and Moses to the close of the Old Testament spanned more than a millennium, with another five hundred years to the close of the New Testament. Still, those portions of the biblical text which have retained their earliest linguistic form (e.g., Exodus 15 and Judges 5) stand in obvious contrast to their literary settings. It is clear that, having begun His written revelation in archaic Hebrew, or more likely in Amorite or some earlier language, God did not hesitate to inspire succeeding biblical authors to change the language forms in order to communicate in the dialects of their day.

Thus, the historical narratives of Samuel and Kings incorporate materials from much older sources such as the royal archives which went all the way back to the time of David (See, e.g., I Kings 11.41 and 14.29). But the historians of Samuel and Kings revised the older sources to read in the Hebrew of the exilic period when these histories of Israel were put into their final form, a revision comparable to putting Wycliffe's translation of the Bible (fourteenth century English) into modern idiom.

The inspired change from Hebrew to Aramaic and then to Greek in the Bible is similar. The earlier Old Testament books were penned in Hebrew. But as Aramaic became the common language of diplomacy and commerce and finally of daily speech in the Eastern Mediterranean and Mesopotamian lands (in the period of the exile), biblical books began to appear in Hebrew heavily influenced by Aramaic, with portions actually in Aramaic, the official language of the Persian empire. The books of Daniel, Ezra, Nehemiah, Esther, and Chronicles especially reflect this adaptation of God to the changing language of His people.

Finally, by the New Testament era Greek had become the most widely used tongue of the biblical world. Given God's demonstrated commitment to communicate His Word in written form intelligible to the generation at hand, the result was predictable. No matter that God had inspired "holy men of old" to write in Hebrew and Aramaic—the Word of His Son would appear in Greek. And not only in Greek, but in *koine*—the "common" Greek of the market place, of the legal documents, of the personal and business correspondence, and even of the world's graffiti. Why? So people could read God's Word in the language of their own day and could understand it as readily as any other contemporary documents.

The question in this section's subtitle is of interest here: "Does God use 'thees' and 'thous'?" The answer is perhaps a surprising but resounding "No!" As a matter of fact, Hebrew, Aramaic, and Greek have no special, "polite" forms of the personal pronouns with which one might address deity or respected persons (unlike German, for instance).

Nor does one find the biblical text preserving *archaic* forms of the personal pronoun in addressing God, although the option was certainly available to the biblical writers. This absence of archaizing pronouns is found throughout the Scripture, in narrative and discourse about God, as well as in prayer and praise to God. The use of English "thy," "thee," and "thou," and related forms in prayer and in some modern Bible translation, is, of course, such an archaizing form of respect. In short, God inspired persons to address Him in the same forms they used to talk to other intimate, contemporary friends, not in any special speech. Why should you study the Bible in your own dialect? For one thing to take seriously the inspired pattern of biblical revelation. God's own commitment to communication commends it.

2. Secondly, you should include a modern English version at or near the center of your Bible study *to keep faith with the passion of the church—the saints' commitment to communication.* Too many heated discussions defending one or another of the historic English versions as the most desirable English Bible for study and depreciating the use of other more recent English versions are divorced from a consideration of the Church's work of preserving and transmitting the written Word of God. (Incidentally, the proper use of the historic versions in study needs no defense!) The passion of God's people to put His Word into the language and dialect of the contemporary readers has from the start led to an almost unending list of revisions and translations. This "translation urge" of the Church was born of the very Spirit of God, as we have seen in the paragraphs above.

The appearance of this compulsion to update the biblical text did not even await the close of the older testament. Thus, while one may point to selected passages which, for one reason or another, have retained their earlier linguistic form, it is not generally so. Spellings were systematically revised, verb and pronominal forms updated. The process of textual revision was already under way before the biblical revelation was finished.

The same may be said for the translation of God's Word. Before the New Testament was even written, all or part of the Old Testament had already been translated into Greek (the Septuagint) and Aramaic (the Targum). Indeed, the Septuagint had itself undergone multiple revision prior to the first Christian century! As if this were not enough, the history of the New Testament's textual transmission is even more awesome. One discovers that before a single syllable of the Bible had appeared in early "English" (late seventh century A.D. for sections in Anglo-Saxon), the New Testament had already been translated in whole or in part into Syriac, Latin, Coptic, Ethiopic, Armenian, Gothic, Georgian, Nubian, and no doubt other tongues as well!

When one turns from such facts to the claims of any one English version to monopolize the believer's attention, one almost feels a sense of shame at the arrogance, if not ignorance, involved. The canonization of any biblical version or revision as the Church's best and last attempt to place the Word of God in the language of the people is a travesty on the labors and sacrifice of saints gone by who gave even their lives in the desire to communicate. Why should you study the Bible in your own dialect? To keep faith with the passion of the church to communicate.

3. Finally, you should study the Scripture in your own tongue *to capitalize on the power of God's Word in your own life—God's communication with you!* If you are to read God's Word with the immediate, contemporary, attention-demanding impact intended by the One who inspired it and supported by the Church which transmitted it, you should study the Bible in your *own* language—not in a foreign tongue, and not in the dialect of your ancestors. In your devotional and study habits as elsewhere in your religious exercises, you must resist

like the plague any language or artificial roles that divorce piety and worship from daily life, from the home and market place, and relegate them to "sacred" places, special times, and esoteric lingo. God does not use "thees" and "thous." Why should you?

KNOW THE BASIC QUESTIONS

Much of what one can learn in specific suggestions about Bible study can be summarized in two basic questions worth memorizing. Answered thoroughly, these questions give significant guidance to a student of the Word.

1. *Question number one: What, as a matter of fact, did the author intend to say to his first readers?* This question takes several important matters into account. First, it asks the reader to recognize the *historical* nature of biblical revelation. The Bible was written over a particular span of history from the late bronze age to the Roman period (roughly 1500 B.C. to 100 A.D.), to specific cultures, customs, and peoples. For example, I and II Kings are not simply a clinical history of Israel preserved for antiquarian interest. Those accounts were penned to the disheartened, disillusioned Jews of the exile (Cf. Psalms 132). They desperately needed an explanation from the Lord as to how the city of God and His temple could possibly have fallen, in view of the promises to David (remember II Samuel 7.8-16?). And Romans was written to imperial Rome, Corinthians to debauched Corinth, and so on.

One must remember then that the Bible was written first to those specific readers, with the Holy Spirit knowing that we would be reading over their shoulder, as it were. So—and this is tremendously important— if one wishes to avoid distorting the biblical message, one must begin by asking what the author intended those first readers to understand, not what he is saying to us. That comes later.

Secondly, the question calls attention to the *objective* nature of the Bible. It is something independent of me, a collection of documents which remain God's Word whether or not I see them. So, the question leads one to the first step in sound Bible study, "Look before you leap." *Look* at what the author actually said before you leap to interpret or apply. *See* what is really there. See the passage clearly. See its details in light of the whole. See it in light of its context. In subsequent chapters we will pursue this important matter of looking—what to look for, how to look. For now it is enough to get the sequence straight. One must see what the author said, all of it, and clearly, before moving to interpret or apply that Word.

Thirdly, the question takes seriously the *authority* of the Scripture. It recalls that the Bible with its message stands independent of me, my tradition, and my preferences. The question cautions one that great care must continually be exercised not to confuse the writers' thoughts with my own.

The question asks concerning the *author's actual* intent. It does not at this point ask concerning what one's church says he said, what the Christian classics say he said, and what the preacher or evangelist said he said, or even what one's parents have said he said, or what one wishes he had said. Rather the question directs the student to take seriously the fact that the Christian disciple lives first under the lordship of Christ and His Word (John 14. 23-24). This does not mean that one is preoccupied with finding "discrepancies" between the Bible and one's church and its documents, the preacher, one's heritage, or even one's own ideas. Nor does it mean that good Bible study is done in isolation, ignoring the church's historic interpretation of the Word. But it surely does mean that Christ and His Word remain to this day judge of all the earth—including *your* church with *all* its personnel and publications, and including your backgrounds and preferences. If that is not true, oft touted cliches about believing the Bible are ridiculous if not blasphemous.

When Christian witness, devotional literature, even well-intentioned counsel or preaching are not seriously evaluated by the Word, frustration and confusion in faith and practice arise. The common understanding, for instance, that anger has no place in the life of the Christian well illustrates that point. Now the Bible clearly insists that a life governed by anger and malice, characterized by inner storm and bitterness is incompatible with life in Christ (Colossians 3.5-10; James 1.19-21), let alone a life of love and full surrender. But it is equally clear that the apostles nowhere envision a person *incapable of anger* at any stage of piety as either possible or desirable. They rather point one to Christ as the model (Ephesians 4.1-16). There one sees the Holy One Himself capable of intense anger (e.g., Mark 3.1-6) but governed by redeeming love (Ephesians 5.1-2).

So it is that Paul's explicit command is not that one never be angry, but rather that one experience anger in such a way and for such reasons as not to lead to sin. "Be angry, but stop sinning (in the process)" (Ephesians 4.26). "Don't nurse your anger overnight" (Ephesians 4.26). Make sure you have a better reason for anger than your own personal inconvenience or mistreatment (I Corinthians 6.1-8). But for heaven's sake, don't ever stand in the presence of real injustice or misrepresentation of the truth with a conscience so limp as to remain unstirred.

"What, as a matter of fact, did the author intend to say to his first readers?" Thus, the first question begins the process of Bible study with *observation,* seeing what the author actually said, and with *interpretation,* seeking to understand what he meant.

2. Now *question number two: What, if anything, does that have to do with us and our world?* This question calls attention to at least two important items which can only be mentioned now and left for more extended comment in subsequent chapters. First, it leads one to come to grips with the fact that not all of the Scripture relates to us in the same way. It is not a matter of the importance of all the Scripture. It is an inescapable question of just how specific passages of the Bible come to bear upon our lives now. Second, it insists that one cannot be content with a purely academic study of the Word, always learning and never coming to a knowledge of the truth and its fantastic significance for the atomic age. So the second question moves on from observation and interpretation to evaluation and application. It is enough now to remember that the Lord of the Scripture will not be content until in some considerable way His Word "becomes flesh" in us (James 1.22-25)!

For more extended treatment of these matters
consult:

Jensen, Irving L. *Independent Bible Study*. Chicago:
  Moody Press, 1963. pp. 17-23, 44-48, 82-106.
Lincoln, William C. *Personal Bible Study*. Minne-
  apolis: Bethany Fellowship, 1975. pp. 13-25.
Traina, Robert A. *Methodical Bible Study*. Wilmore,
  KY: The Author, 1952. pp. v-26.

Recurring reference will be made to these fine texts at
the end of each chapter. Of the three, Robert Traina's
Methodical Bible Study is the most exhaustive. While it
is a technically written, college and seminary text, it is
within the grasp of lay persons accustomed to reading and
to analytical thought. Irving Jensen's *Independent Bible
Study* and William Lincoln's *Personal Bible Study* are
both non-technical, popular treatments, with obvious debt
to Dr. Traina's work. Of the two, Lincoln's book is, on
the whole, preferable in this writer's opinion. Still Jensen's
work is helpful and will be used with profit.

CHAPTER II

LOOK BEFORE YOU LEAP

Suppose you want to answer that first basic question, "What, as a matter of fact, did the author intend to say to his first readers?" Begin by looking carefully at what he wrote. "Look at what the author said before you leap to interpret and apply!" So, assuming a context of prayer, the first step in good Bible study is *observation*. And one must see two things. First, one must see *what is there*; this is a matter of the *contents*. That is what the book or segment at hand is actually about: sin or grace, prayer or faith, Abraham or David, creation or second coming. These are matters of content, of observing *what* was said. Second, one must see *how* what is there is there; this is a matter of *structure*. That is how the material is arranged, tied together. So one begins by seeing what is there and how it goes together.

STUDY IN UNITS

Few disciplines will revolutionize your Bible study more than this: "Study in units!" The reason is obvious. When you read the Bible in this way, you begin to see through the eyes of the author. Most of the biblical books were penned finally as units, regardless of the history of various sources used by the writers. It was assumed that every section would be understood in light of the whole.

27

Reading the book of Jonah, for example, one will ponder the implications of Jonah's flight from God in chapter one. But the insights will be limited at best unless the reflection takes seriously into account the *last* chapter of the book. There Jonah gives the reason for his "escape" from God in the first place—a deep seated disagreement with God's mercy, if it included the hated Ninevites too (4.2ff.). His disobedience and running from God were far more than quibbling over a call. He had a basic argument with God. Only one who sees the book as a whole will uncover that, and yet it is a main point of the book.

Aim at seeing books as wholes. At the very least, begin to see chapters as collections of related paragraphs whose main points form an intelligent whole. Give attention to individual verses only as you may see them in light of the paragraph and chapter in which they are set. Start this discipline now!

Use an edition of the Bible printed in paragraph units rather than one that sets each verse apart as a unit standing on its own, a misleading "verse paragraph." If you have never attempted the study of the Bible by larger units, begin with a more basic book (Mark or Galatians before Esther or Ecclesiastes) and a smaller book (Mark or Colossians before Acts or Revelation), or simply a section of a book.

Reading in units makes use of different "study lenses" in sequence. First the *wide-angle* lens to get the big picture. Second the *close-up* lens to look carefully at the parts that compose the larger picture. And last the wide-angle again to see the unit as a panorama once more, now with greater perception after detailed exposure to the parts. We will give attention here to the first phase, since that facet of Bible study is rarely used by non-professionals.

Look Before you Leap

SEE WHAT IS THERE: THE CONTENT

The following suggestions are extremely useful in beginning to see what is actually in the unit selected for study.

1. *Survey the unit.* Read the book or set of chapters through quickly to get an overview. You will have to work at this if your pace has been verse by verse. Read the unit this way (several times, if possible), observing persons, places, and themes of *overall importance.* Note them (pen and paper!) for further study.

2. *Title each chapter/paragraph.* On one of these survey readings give titles to each chapter, to each paragraph also if your book is five to six chapters or less. Use imagination here and don't underestimate the value of this exercise. Short titles (three to five words), information-packed are best. Make them memorable and don't worry about what someone else might think of them. These titles put handles on the entire book or segment in an amazing way. Try it!

3. *Note proportions and sense the atmosphere.* Without getting bogged down in detail, note how much space is devoted to each item in your unit. Stick with major features here. In Jonah, for example, one would note the surprising amount of space devoted to the prophet's attitude problem—one entire chapter in four! And one would sense the shift from Jonah's helpless tone in chapter two to the sullen, argumentative mood of chapter four. What a change of atmosphere!

4. *Observe the literary type.* Is the book written in prose or poetry (or both)? Most modern translations set poetry off with indented lines to help you spot this shift.

Is the unit a narrative of history or events, a letter, a legal code, a prophecy, a song, a prayer, an essay? It may make a difference in how you interpret some of its materials.

5. *Draw a picture* of your unit, using a rough chart and incorporating your chapter/paragraph titles and any other survey information you can. Here are two simple samples:

"Jonah: Prophet Running From God's Mercy"
(Book as a whole)

Jonah's flight from God 1.1 16	Jonah's prayer from the fish 17 2.10	Nineveh repents, God relents 3.1 10	Jonah angry at mercy 4.1 11

"Mark 2.1-3.6: Controversial Christ"
(Segment as a whole)

Who can forgive sins? 2.1 12	Why eat with sinners? 13 17	Why not fast? 18 22	Why not on Sabbath? 23 3.6

Relevant information about time, place, main persons, etc., can be conveniently placed beneath the appropriate section title on a chart like this.

So much for seeing what is there and doing it in units. We must turn now to the second feature of the observation process, seeing the structure.

LOOK FOR THE DESIGN: THE RELATIONSHIPS

A story can be told any number of ways. How it is put together is a matter of design—in the Bible, inspired design. The fact that a given biblical unit begins as it does, proceeds and ends as it does, develops the themes, poses the questions and answers, presents the causes, effects, climaxes, contrasts, and comparisons that it does, as it does, are all a matter of the inspired author's choice. The discovery of that design (the literary structure) is the reader's task. Its study returns lavish dividends.

That the biblical authors structured their writings with design arising out of their respective purposes is obvious in the gospel writers' presentations of Jesus. The four evangelists begin the story four different ways: Matthew with a genealogy and infancy narrative through Joseph's eyes, Mark with the ministry of John and Jesus' baptism (without reference to the birth of either), Luke with the conception of John and Jesus and the latter's youth, and John with a prologue introducing Jesus as the eternal, divine Word become flesh. John plainly says he selected (and apparently also arranged) his materials according to an overall purpose (John 20:30-31). These differences are a matter of inspired choice, not literary chance. The more students see this and study it, the more they think the writer's thoughts after him. Try the following suggestions in your Bible study and watch yourself leave superficial reading behind!

1. *Learn the basic structural relationships.* Discovering the design (the structure) of a biblical unit is simply seeing how its various parts fit together. One's skill in perceiving how an author has put his work together can be greatly increased by learning the basic relationships used by writers in structuring their compositions. The following concepts should become stock in trade study tools for the serious Bible student, for they are standard literary tools of all authors, including those inspired by the Holy Spirit. Start by learning the following relationships.

a. *Cause-effect relationships.* When A produces B they are in a cause-effect relationship. Thus in John 3.16 God's love is the cause; sending the Son is the effect. In that same context belief and unbelief are contrasting causes, each having their own effects. Sometimes the effect precedes, followed by the cause as in Romans 1.16: "I am not ashamed of the Good News about Christ [the effect], because it is God's power unto salvation to every person who believes" [the cause]. Cause-effect is causation; effect-cause is substantiation. Connecting words like "for," "because," "since" are clues here.

b. *Climax.* A series of elements developing in a crescendo of feeling, of importance, or of intensity to a final high point form a climax. So Hosea's work begins with the major comparison depicting God's love in Hosea's parable marriage (Hosea, 1-3). But then again in chapter 6 (The Dilemma of God's Love) and chapter 11 (The History of God's love) the subject of Yahweh's love reappears, moving with increasing urgency to the climactic, unexpected Invitation of Love in the closing chapter (Hosea 14). This book of judgment is designed to end in a climax of divine love. Think of it! Can you find the climax in the book of Jonah?

c. *Comparison.* Here one item is laid beside another to illustrate or illuminate it. Often "like" or "as" are used. In Psalm 103.13 the Lord's pity for those who fear Him is illuminated by comparison to a father's attitude toward his children—that's the sort of heart God has. The major comparison of the harlot, Gomer, to Israel, and the loving Hosea to God in Hosea 1-3, has been noted already. What important comparison do you recall from the Lord's Prayer (Matthew 6.12)?

d. *Contrast.* Here *opposite* items are set side by side. What contrasts do you see in John 3.16? In Romans 6.23? Jonah, chapter 4, is structured by a basic contrast throughout. Two opposing sets of attitudes are carefully put side by side by the author. What are they, and what do they involve? Pursue it; you'll be amazed. "But" is the common clue word here.

e. *Cruciality (the pivot).* A passage that takes a major turn, reversing a previous course, is said to be structured by cruciality. II Samuel is so designed, with the turning point set clearly in chapter 11. Just look at 11.27b. Pow! *To* that point the writer presents the rise of David's house, *from* that point its decline, and *at* that point the crux of the reversal—David's sin with Bathsheba *and* God's attitude toward it. One can usually see causes producing the drastic contrasts involved here.

f. *Generalization/particularization.* When the author moves *from* a *specific* statement *to* a more *general* saying on the same subject he *generalizes.* Doing the reverse, moving *from* a *general to* a more *restricted* statement, he particularizes. Matthew 5.17-48 is structured by particularization. Jesus' general statements about fulfilling the law (5.17) and righteousness exceeding that of the scribes and Pharisees (5.20) are followed by six, more specific examples of how this fulfillment and true righteousness are to be understood (5.21-26, 27-30, 31-32, 33-37, 38-42, and 43-48). What particularizations follow and explain the general statement in Matthew 6.1? Find them and relate them to 6.1.

g. *Introduction.* Passages which prepare the way for the presentation that follows are introductory. Thus the dramatic cycle of speeches in Job is introduced by chapters one and two which emphasize the wealth and piety of Job and the origin of his ills in his goodness rather than in any sin.

h. *Question-answer (problem-solution).* Many biblical passages are structured by the presentation of a question with its answer(s) or a problem with its solution(s). The Book of Exodus is designed this way. Problems are presented in chapters 1-5 to which the plagues, the Exodus, the covenant, and the tabernacle are God's solutions. Look at Mark 7 and Matthew 24 in this way and see what you find.

i. *Recurrence.* Recurrence is the reappearance of words, phrases, ideas, themes, structures, or other elements, whether the same or slightly altered. Recurrence is used to develop emphases and motifs in a unit and is one of the most common tools used to structure biblical materials. See how the prophet Amos used recurrence to tie his introductory indictments together effectively while zeroing in on Israel in Amos 1.3-2.8.

2. *Find the Design.* Knowing that authors use the sorts of relationships listed above to tie their materials together, read the Bible looking for them. Read with structure in mind, whether your unit is large or small. These

relationships are most easily discerned between small units like phrases or clauses. See these, but aim also to see those structures that bind large amounts of material together, such as the contrast running throughout the whole of Jonah, chapter 4, or the problem-solution design that unites the whole book of Exodus. The writer put the material together in the way he felt most effective. Don't miss it! Look until you think you see what his design was.

Remember the cruciality by which II Samuel is structured (see e, above)? There is no particular reason why the writer could not have introduced the entire story of David's royal family with an observation in chapter one that its destiny hinged largely on the "royal affair" with Bathsheba. But he did not. Instead, there is not the slightest hint that this event, clinically recounted in chapter eleven, spells disaster for the king. After all, kings can do as they please, can they not? But then one comes to those closing lines of II Samuel 11. That fact must be observed to catch the real punch of the book. Look for structure!

3. *Probe Relationships.* Don't stop with the *observation* of an author's literary design. Go on to probe these relationships with questions focusing both on the structure itself and on the specific materials as arranged by the writer. In Matthew 5, for example, one must not stop with the discovery that most of the chapter is built around the specific statements growing out of Jesus' more general sayings on fulfilling the law, and righteousness exceeding that of the scribes and the Pharisees (particularization). One must press on to ask questions. What do the general statements about fulfilling the law and righteousness exceeding that of the scribes and Pharisees really mean?

What do each of the related particularizations mean—being angry with the brother and saying "you fool" (5.22), looking lustfully (5.28), divorce and unchastity (5.32), not swearing at all (5.34), not resisting evil (5.39), and loving your enemies (5.44)? What did Jesus and Matthew really intend by each of these? Why were these general statements the first major focus after the introduction to this address as Matthew records it? Why are they expounded by these particular examples? How does each of the more specific paragraphs give meaning to the concepts of fulfilling the law and righteousness beyond that of the scribes and Pharisees? What does all this imply?

These are sample questions to which you can find answers if you study the passage and reflect prayerfully on it. The point is this: when you have seen something in the Bible (here a relationship), don't leave it there. Press on to probe it for meaning, using questions to be answered by further study. More on this in the next chapter, however. For now, get started *looking* for *what* the author said and *how* he said it in the Bible unit you have chosen to study.

For further study:

Jensen. *Independent Bible Study.* pp. 27-43, 49-72, 106-113.

Lincoln. *Personal Bible Study.* pp. 27-66.

Traina. *Methodical Bible Study.* pp. 31-88.

CHAPTER III

ASK QUESTIONS AND FIND ANSWERS

Asking and answering questions is the bridge that joins seeing what the author said (observation) and understanding what he meant (interpretation). The process is so important that it merits separate attention as a major step in Bible study that works.

LEARN STANDARD QUESTIONS TO
GET AT MEANING

Most persons know the quips about "Who? what? where? when? why? and how?" but do not exploit their full potential in Bible study. Wise Bible students will learn the *set types of questions* which need to be asked and will address them to every major matter they observe in the text. They will give attention as well to the sort of information they seek through the questions.

The most important standard questions are the following. Ask questions to get *definition*: Who or what is this? What is the meaning or significance of this? Ask questions to learn *reasons*: Why is this so? What is the purpose? Ask questions to understand the *means*: How is this done? And explore *implications* and assumptions with questions: What is implied by this? What does this assume? Ask the other questions regarding place and time as they are appropriate.

Don't assume too readily that you know what the text means. Observing that Jesus said one must be "born again" to "see the Kingdom of God" (John 3.3) is one thing; knowing what Jesus meant is another. Of course we know, or think we do, what modern evangelists mean by being "born again"; we know what current pamphlets mean by the phrase. But what did Jesus mean by it in the first century A.D., talking to a Jew who had never heard "accepting Christ as Savior" or "becoming a Christian" or other standard expressions now associated with the phrase?

Don't allow these and other questions to float distractingly around in your mind. Rather write them down for reference, rephrasing them to get at the specific materials you are studying. Record as many questions as you can from as many different angles as possible on a specific passage. Just the asking sharpens your perception of the depth and breadth of a passage. The answers will give you the meaning.

QUESTION MAJOR MATTERS FIRST

Attend to major matters first and to details only as they relate to the whole. Here is where the previous observation of the unit as a whole and of its inspired design can be of great help. This will generally mean focusing questions first on the materials as you have seen them to be structured. For if you see how the author put together a whole unit and then focus your questions there, you will not become bogged down in chasing peripheral matters. Rather you will pursue matters of overall importance to the unit's meaning and the author's own emphasis.

This will generally mean *focusing questions first on structure*. For example, if you observe that Jonah 4 presents throughout the whole chapter a major contrast between Jonah's attitude and God's, don't let the matter drop there. Proceed to explore that discovery with your "tool kit" of standard questions. Then look for answers as you are able. Work right through the various types of questions you should ask. Address questions of *definition* to this insight concerning the contrast: What are the aspects of Jonah's attitude and of God's which are set forth here? What is involved in each? What is the meaning of each of the major terms used in the presentation, e.g., Jonah's anger and God's compassion and pity? How do they differ from one another? What is the basic, deep-down contrast?

Ask for reasons guided by the structure: Why does the writer present this contrast? Why present it here at the end of the book? Why does Jonah's attitude differ so completely from God's? Why does God pursue the question of Jonah's anger? Why in the manner chosen?

Ask for implications: What does the contrast here in attitudes imply? What does the author assume about Jonah's motives? About God's? What is implied by the fact that the book ends with this contrast? What is implied about the nature of obedience? About the nature of God? About the value of persons? About the sin of bigotry and the gravity of selfishness by this stark contrast?

Or again, when you see that Mark 2.1-3.6 is designed to bring together a series of important questions addressed to Jesus on major aspects of his person and work, don't drop the matter there. Go on to pursue this question-answer structure with adaptations of your standard questions, and you will rapidly get beneath the surface of this unit.

So, guided by your structural observations, ask for *definitions*: In each of these paragraphs, what really is the main question posed, and what really is the answer given to each? How does each answer reply to the question asked? What is the meaning of the most significant words in the main questions and in their answers?

Address questions about *reasons* regarding this collection of questions-answers: Why were these questions asked about Jesus' person, His works, His worship, His understanding of law? Why did Jesus answer in each case as He did? Why are these questions and answers brought together in this way for the reader? Why placed here at the outset of Mark's presentation of Jesus?

Ask for *implications*: What is implied by each of these questions and answers? Implied about the writer's concerns? About the people's understanding of Jesus? About Jesus' understanding of Himself? What is implied about the nature of worship? About the meaning of keeping the law? About the import of the Sabbath for Jesus' disciples?

Do you see the pattern? Don't get side-tracked in discussing the architecture of the tiled roof in 2.1-12 or the precise type of grain in 2.18-26. They are important only as you do more detailed study. The questions and the answers were apparently the author's main concern, so focus your attention there. Then ask whatever other questions you wish when you have finished dealing with the main concerns of the passage.

Not only is there a stock set of questions which every interpreter of the word should have ready to ask at a moment's notice; but there is also something of an order to follow in both asking and in answering the questions. Like other matters of Bible study this order should not rigidly confine creative work, but should serve as a guide to proper interpretation. The order: first definition, then reasons, means, implications, and other questions. The reason is obvious. One cannot well reflect on why something is, or what it implies, until one knows what it is. To return to John 3, one cannot say very well why Jesus said one must be "born again" or what is implied by it unless one knows what the phrase actually means. Begin with definition, the who and what questions.

FIND ANSWERS

1. *In the context.* Many people ask questions but then either simply make up answers based on their past experience or immediately consult an expert's opinion in a commentary or Bible encyclopedia. Some questions of geography, history, and culture, and definitions of some words are best answered in one of these secondary sources, when you have seen what you can in the text. The following works are examples of the excellent resources available to help the student find information on such matters:

Douglas, J.D., (ed.). *The New Bible Dictionary.* London: Inter-Varsity Fellowship, 1962.

Tenny, Merrill C. (ed.). *The Zondervan Pictorial Encyclopedia of the Bible.* 5 vols. Grand Rapids: Zondervan, 1975.

Unger, Merrill F. *Unger's Bible Dictionary*. Chicago: Moody Press, 1959.

So, for example, the question in Mark 2.16 regarding Jesus' association with "sinners and tax collectors" is clarified by the meaning of these terms in their historical setting. There one would discover that the Pharisees classified all persons who did not keep Pharisaic tradition as "sinners," not simply persons who disobeyed Mosaic law. One would also learn of the graft and corruption almost inherent in the consignment system of collection under which the revenue agents of both Herod and Rome worked, so that a tax collector was universally assumed to be "on the take" and ranked with thieves and murderers in Jewish tradition. The boldness of Jesus' lifestyle and the force of the Pharisees' question emerge clearly with such information. You can find it in a Bible dictionary or encyclopedia.

But many important questions can be satisfactorily answered from the immediate context or the larger context of the whole book or related passages in other biblical books. That is why this section says, "*Find* answers!" *You* look for them. They are there.

For instance, when you study Mark 3.28 on Jesus' statement about "blasphemy against the Holy Spirit" and "an eternal sin" which "never has forgiveness," the place to look first for a definition of what "blasphemy" might mean is in the immediate context. There the attitudes and conduct of the persons referred to by Jesus are clearly shown (Mark 3.19b-27).

The persons involved were well acquainted with the Hebrew Scriptures and had apparently come from Jerusalem for the very purpose of observing Jesus. They had evidently seen His works and knew His claims. They categorically rejected Jesus and His teaching as having anything to do with God and good. He is of the devil, they said. There was far more at issue here than a few words passed between them and Jesus, merely a so-called "taking the Holy Spirit's name in vain." A whole mind-set (review Mark 2.1-3.6) and way of life was expressed in their derision of Jesus. That, said Jesus, was blasphemy against the Holy Spirit and would never be forgiven. The answer from the context is more illuminating than one you will dream up by mere reflection on preaching or testimony.

At the end of this same chapter (Mark 3) Jesus says that "whoever does the will of God" is His true relative. One will certainly ask what He meant by the will of God (definition). What does one do who lives God's will? Go to the context. Start with that series of questions and answers in Mark 2.1-3.6. There God's will as reflected in His Son was stated on four major issues of life in the Kingdom of God. There you will find God's will on forgiveness (2.1-12), on ministry by association (2.13-17), on the place of religious observance in the disciples' life (2.18-22), and on the priority of compassionate action over legalistic observance of law (2.23-3.6). There from the context is an excellent start on the answer to your question. Or perhaps the immediate context of the paragraph setting is all that is necessary in this case to define "doing the will of the Father." Here Jesus may simply be referring to persons who receive Him and listen eagerly to His teaching. If so, those who "do the will of the Father" would be those who wish to know and understand His way, as opposed to the scribes in 3.21 ff., who have already rejected Jesus as an imposter.

2. *In major terms.* Almost always, questions of definition will involve the identification and the understanding of the major terms of a unit. For example, discovering the meaning of the contrasted attitudes in Jonah 4 would surely involve an understanding of the terms "anger," "compassion," and "pity" which appear to be important to that passage. Understanding Jesus' statement on the "unforgiveable sin" will be enhanced by definition of the term "blasphemes," which is at the heart of His veiled accusation against the scribes in Mark 3.29.

These word definitions can also be found in Bible dictionaries and encyclopedias mentioned before. But many times serious Bible students would be better informed to do their own study of the word, for Bible words, like our own, are best defined by their use, not by a simple "dictionary definition." In order to study the use of a biblical word, two pieces of information are necessary: 1) the biblical references where the word appears, and 2) the identification of the Greek or Hebrew term translated by the word you are studying. The biblical references are necessary of course simply to find the uses of the word. The identification of the Greek or Hebrew word is necessary to guarantee that one is studying a single word and not different words which happen to be translated by the same English term.

It is well known, for example, that in the Authorized Version (KJV) of the New Testament the English word "perfect" translates three different Greek words, which have only superficial relationship to each other and are distinctly different words, from different backgrounds, with different emphases. Thus, the student studying 2 Timothy 3.17, "That the man of God may be *perfect,* thoroughly furnished unto all good works," will be misinformed if he or she relates this use directly to the set of occurrences where "the perfect" are contrasted with immature persons (e.g., in 1 Corinthians 2.6; Ephesians 4.13ff.) where a second Greek word is used, or to Luke 1.3 where still a third word underlies the translation "perfect." The word translated "perfect" in 2 Timothy 3.17 has to do with fitness, preparedness, being equipped for a job. The second word used by Paul or others has to do with being grown up (usually in Christ and defined by love). The third word, used by the historian Luke, has to do with accuracy. None of these words is related to the others. While some more recent versions will help the student avoid confusion in these particular instances, the problem is inherent in translation and will arise no matter what version one uses. Examples could be multiplied almost endlessly.

But resources are available which allow the student both to locate the places where the word under study appears and to avoid confusion with other similarly translated words. These resources are of two types: analytical concordances and so-called "Englishman's" concordances. The following are recommended:

Strong, James. *Exhaustive Concordance of the Bible.* 1890. Reprint. Nashville: Abingdon Press, 1973.

Wigram, George V. *The Englishman's Greek Concordance.* 1903. Reprint. Grand Rapids: Zondervan, 1972.

Wigram, George V. *The Englishman's Hebrew and Chaldee Concordance of the Old Testament.* 1890. Reprint. Grand Rapids: Zondervan, 1972.

Young, Robert. *Analytical Concordance of the Bible.* Revised ed., 1936. Reprint. Grand Rapids: Eerdmans, n.d.

The use of each work is explained in its introduction. A half-hour spent learning to use any of these tools is time well invested.

CHECK YOUR ANSWERS

How can one know whether or not the conclusions drawn in answer to interpretive questions are sound? Many questions, of course, do not have clear cut answers. Answers with "probably" and "perhaps" are sufficient and often helpful. But there are important check points, some already implied in the preceding materials, by which one may evaluate proposed answers to questions raised regarding the meaning of a passage and its parts. Some of these check points reside in the text and its setting and are not under the control of the interpreter. Others are within the interpreter or his or her observed or shared experience. They are all important[1]

1. *Word form and meaning.* Acceptable answers must conform to the observed form and meaning of a word or expression in its context, apart from the preference of the interpreter. Thus, for instance, Paul's statement in Ephesians 2.8 must include the meaning of accomplished, *present* salvation. The statement reads: "By grace *you are* saved through faith." While Paul elsewhere talks of the process of salvation (e.g., I Corinthians 2.18) and of the future completion of God's saving work (e.g., Romans 8:18-25), here Paul asserts that the Ephesian Christians are *now* in some sense saved. The English ex-

46

pression is present perfect, describing a present condition, a fine translation of the Greek perfect which here lies behind it. The interpreter is here hemmed in by the form/ inflection of the word (present perfect, not future, not past or present continuing).

Furthermore, the context here in Ephesians 2 is consistent with Paul's use of the word elsewhere, leading to the conclusion that "saved" must here have to do with a *gracious rescue* from the personal and social consequences of sin, a transfer from death in sin to life in Christ, out of alienation from God to fellowship with Him and His people. "Saved" does not mean merely to be "forgiven," or to be "acquitted" or "loved." The use of the word here and elsewhere simply will not allow it, but rather points in a different direction. The interpreter can check answers then by the forms of words and their meanings as determined by etymology and especially by use.

2. *Context.* Suggested interpretations of a text must conform to the flow of thought in the context. Consider I Corinthians 2.9 (KJV): "Eye hath not seen, nor ear heard, neither have entered into the heart of man, the things which God hath prepared for them that love him." The context shows that, contrary to much popular misunderstanding, the apostle is not here speaking of the unknown glories of the new heaven. The paragraphs around this text make it clear that Paul was not quoting Isaiah 64:4 to talk about what we do not know, but, on the contrary, to affirm what we do know.

The thought-flow is clear: (a) Paul preached at Corinth only the simple gospel of Christ crucified (vv. 1-5): (b) nevertheless among more mature believers elsewhere he taught "a secret and hidden wisdom of God" (vv. 6-7):

(c) this wisdom was beyond the comprehension of the power people of this world (v.8); (d) but, and here is the point of the famous quote, "What no eye has ever seen" *on its own,* "God *has revealed* to us through the Spirit" (v. 10)! Paul then proceeds to explain that the problem lay not in his inability to teach more than the basic gospel principles, nor in the Holy Spirit's ability to show mankind the deep mind of God, but rather in the Corinthians' own immaturity which prevented their grasp of more exalted instruction (2.11-3.4).

This text then is a statement about the amazing fact of God's ability to reveal Himself and His will to us by His Spirit, and about the inability of people on their own to comprehend God's wisdom. And it arises in a discussion of the need for Christian maturity. Context is the test of interpretation here and always.

3. *Author's intent.* The significance of a passage must agree with the author's intent, as best it can be determined. Thus St. John says, "By this we know love, that He laid down His life for us; and we ought to lay down our lives for the brethren. But if any one has the world's goods and sees his brother in need, yet closes his heart against him, how does God's love abide in him?" (I John 3.16-17). John's statement enjoins love *between* members of the Christian community ("brethren"). While this is true, to use this statement as a basis for *confining* Christian love to fellow members of the Christian community would be a terrible misreading of the spirit of the apostle and a misuse of his writing. Elsewhere in this work John stresses the universal reach of Christ's redeeming life and death (I John 2.2) and God's example of loving us before we love Him (I John 4.10 and 19), surely indicating a stance which

makes it difficult to conclude that John intended love to be calculating and confined in any way. To cite another, more obvious example in this letter, interpretation of John's statements regarding sin and its confession in this work must take into account his clear statement of purpose in 2.2: "My little children, I am writing this to you so that you may not sin."

4. *Historical setting.* It is a constant temptation to forget that the cultural setting of the biblical writers differed significantly from ours. We tend to think first of our own customs and assume those referred to in the Bible were similar, when they were often otherwise. Meanings suggested for passages must fit their historical setting. We have already seen an example of this in the "publicans" of Mark 2.16. Thus these "publicans" were "tax collectors," as the RSV and other recent versions make clear. But even so they were not revenue agents of the type known to persons in modern democratic societies, a sort of ancient IRS personnel. Rather they collected taxes under a consignment arrangement that fostered incredible graft. As a result, pious Jews ranked tax collectors with thieves and murderers. No wonder Jesus' association with them was questioned!

Context, word form, word meaning, author's intent, and the historical setting are matters external to modern interpreters and beyond their control, even though their discovery involves judgment on their part. Some other significant checks for interpretive answers are found within the interpreters' experience or that of other persons.

5. *Spiritual discernment.* This is a sense born not so much of age as of prolonged exposure to the Scripture and

sincere, deepening association with the living Word Himself. It is an ability to discern the "ring of truth" in an interpretation that goes beyond data and evidence to intuition born of the Spirit of God. It is this sense by God's Spirit that has safeguarded the mass of interpreters in the life of the Church who, though untutored in technical biblical interpretation have lived devoted to God through Christ. The resulting consensus of interpretation in the history of the Church is amazing, the many divergent viewpoints notwithstanding.

6. *Common sense.* This check calls the interpreter to stick to the most obvious meaning of a text and reject hidden or overly subtle meanings proposed. Hyperbolic and figurative expressions are taken as such. Overly technical interpretations are excluded from material not intended for technical understanding, say in biology or botany (cf. Jesus' words about the "mustard seed," Mark 4.31), allowing the biblical writers the freedom to communicate which we ourselves require.

7. *Experience.* The interpreter's own experience is not the final arbiter of Scripture. On the one hand, the fact that I have not yet witnessed a resurrection from the dead does not allow me either to deny the reality of such an occurrence or to redefine the word. At the same time, biblical interpretation must match life as we experience it. This should caution the interpreter against making Jesus' statement, "If you abide in me, and my words abide in you, ask whatever you will, and it shall be done for you" (John 15.7), an unqualified promise regarding positive answer to prayer. The experience of Jesus Himself and of the apostles, along with that of the devout of the Church, leads to the conclusion that a qualification is implicit.

In this case the test of experience should lead the student back to the context and the text itself to a more careful consideration of qualifications actually present there.

So then, by looking carefully in the immediate and the larger context, by studying the use of significant terms both on one's own and with the help of secondary sources, answers to questions can be found. And tests of one's interpretive answers can lead in the end to sound understandings of the Word of God.

Actual *lack of ability* will seldom thwart persons seeking to discover the meaning of Scripture. More often they will stumble over one of two opposing hurdles. On the one hand, some will ask many questions and then will *assume* they cannot find answers, since they are not specialists. They will fail to hear the Word significantly because they underestimate their own ability to see and understand, and because they fail to use resources available to help in the search for answers. On the other hand, others will fail to ask questions, naively assuming they already understand the Scripture. Or they will fail to look for answers, thinking they already have all the answers. They will substitute traditional and abbreviated, and often very distorted understandings of the Scripture, for an authentic understanding of the Word based on personal inquiry and openness to the Spirit. Either mistake is a tragedy. Others—"and these are those who hear the Word"—will not only observe and ask questions, but will proceed to find answers. They will discover that Jesus spoke the truth: "The words that I have spoken to you are spirit and life" (John 6.63).

For further study:

Jensen. *Independent Bible Study.* pp. 72-74, 133-158, though in many ways Jensen's presentation of the question asking/answering process is weak. The "analytical chart" tool developed by Jensen may be sufficiently different from the presentation used here to make the connections with the present study difficult to observe for the beginning student.

Lincoln. *Personal Bible Study.* pp. 69-108.

Traina. *Methodical Bible Study.* pp. 89-200.

---

[1]The following discussion owes considerable debt to Robert Traina's discussion of "Determinants of Interpretive Answers," *Methodical Bible Study*, pp. 135-165. Dr. Traina's distinction between "subjective determinants" (spiritual sense, common sense, and experience) and "objective determinants" and his recognition of the validity and importance of the so-called "subjective determinants" is particularly helpful.

CHAPTER IV

LET JESUS BE THE JUDGE

Just how the Bible is to be applied to the atomic age is a topic of great debate. No matter how it is done, some process of evaluation must be used in weighing the biblical passages to be applied. All biblical interpreters, professional and lay, engage in this evaluation process whether they know it or not, deny it or not. No one lives by all the Bible's teachings without exception. Simply to say that one must "take the Bible literally" will not do, for all of us are selective in the passages we take as mandates for our own lifes. We must recognize this and attempt to be consistent, and more important, faithful to the intent of biblical revelation in our very selection.

When one speaks of evaluating biblical texts it is not a question of importance or unimportance of any part of biblical revelation. It is rather a question, and sometimes a difficult one, as to just how specific passages are to be related to our setting, at least nineteen centuries removed from the original writing and culture.

The following guidelines for evaluation arise from the nature of the biblical materials themselves. Though by no means exhaustive, they can help increase the consistency and perceptiveness with which one lives the Bible in today's world.

KEEP THE SACRED STORY STRAIGHT

Remember that the Scripture was written over a period of at least twelve hundred years. During those centuries and many preceding ones described in the Bible, God patiently taught people of Himself, of His ways, and of how they might live with Him by faith. Pacing Himself partly by His creatures' ability to understand the truth and partly by His agenda for their instruction, God nurtured them as a father would a child, as Hosea expressly says (Hosea 11.3). This is why the first "Sermon on the Mount" was the Mosaic law and not the discourse of Jesus on perfection in love (Matthew 5.44-48). This fact was well known to the New Testament writers (Hebrews 1.1ff.).

When one is reading the Old Testament particularly, he must remember that the passage at hand may not have been God's last word on the subject. Subsequent biblical revelation may have refined, revised, or even rescinded the instruction one is now studying. This must be considered before one sets out to "live the Word" in this instance. The Levitical laws of sacrifice and ceremony are obvious examples of passages whose direct application to the twentieth century Christian would often be impossible and usually pointless. But there are also important instances of moral and spiritual teaching which are inadequate without reference to later instruction by the Father.

In order to keep the story of biblical revelation straight one needn't master all the details of Old and New Testament history. Begin by learning the major periods of biblical history—patriarchal, Mosaic, conquest, united monarchy, divided monarchy, exile, restoration, life of Christ, and apostolic period—and the centuries or decades covered by each. Any standard Bible dictionary or encyclopedia will provide summary articles on Old and New Testament history. Some study Bibles have excellent introductory essays on this subject. Study these and make your own chronological chart, noting major events and persons. Give particular attention to correlating prophetic and apostolic writings with their settings as presented in the historical writings of the testaments. Kings and Acts respectively are important in this regard. For example, put Amos in the decadent, final decades of the Northern Kingdom and I Corinthians in the light of the setting given in Acts 18.

SEPARATE THE LOCAL FROM THE UNIVERSAL

Separate what is of local, historically limited significance from what is of universal significance by penetrating beneath the surface to the principle being addressed in each passage. Probe to the underlying issue with which the passage deals. To acquire some idea of the principles which are foundational in biblical faith, one should become conversant with those passages which, by the obvious structure of the books and the express statements of the authors involved, are treatments of God's highest will for humanity or are outlines of life in the Kingdom. Such passages include Matthew 5-7, Romans 12-24, I Corinthians 13, Ephesians 4.1-16, Colossians 3.12ff., Philippians 2, and others. Incidentally, the minimal amount of culture-bound material in these passages is striking. Here it becomes obvious that in the process of evaluation both of biblical passages and of proposed interpretations one should:

a. Take the personal over the mechanical.
b. Take liberty over legalism.
c. Take faith over works.
d. Take love over all else.

These preferences surface continually, not only in the great outlines of God's highest designs for His people noted above, but again and again like threads in a tapestry throughout the entire Scripture.

Thus, if some proposed interpretation of Scripture propounds an application of holiness that is not loving, neither is it an adequate understanding of biblical holiness. Biblical interpretations and applications must be rejected if they render one's walk with God more mechanical than personal. If they make one more dependent on external conformity to isolated biblical phrases than on dynamic relationship with God, the interpretations and applications are deficient. They simply do not reflect the deepest biblical concerns. In short, one has missed the point of the Bible!

LET JESUS BE THE JUDGE

When asking whether the actions and attitudes modeled or commended in any specific part of the Scripture are to be applied to the life of the Christian, evaluate them by the standard of Jesus' life and words. This principle is supported by two facts. First, Jesus clearly presented Himself as Lord of all revelation (e.g., He authoritatively revised the revelation through Moses, Mark 10.4ff., Matthew 5.21-48). Second, the apostles clearly wrote taking Jesus as the norm for life in the Kingdom (e.g., Philippians 2).

Thus, reading Psalm 139, one may model the Psalmist's clear renunciation of evil and decisive dedication to God (139.21-22). But one may not hate evil persons, or anyone for that matter. The "perfect" hatred in verse 22 is "complete" hatred, not somehow "acceptable." That was perhaps adequate for the Psalmist, but not for disciples of Jesus, as the Master and the apostles clearly state (Matthew 5 again and Romans 12). There is no "contradiction" between the Psalmist's attitudes and those taught by Jesus, but there is a chasm of several centuries in which the Father taught us more perfectly His will.

Recognizing such updates in revelation, seeing the differences, and selecting the higher way for application to the life of the Christian is precisely what is involved constantly in deciding what and how the lifegiving Word will be lived out in our day. Let Jesus be the judge. That will not end all questions, but it will go a long way toward helping one evaluate biblical passages consistently.

For further study:
Lincoln. *Personal Bible Study.* pp. 111-116.
Traina. *Methodical Bible Study.* pp. 201-213.

CHAPTER V

LIVE THE WORD

RAISE THE "SO WHAT?" QUESTION

Living the Word: This is the goal of the entire process. Good Bible study is much more than an academic pursuit. Its goal is human transformation by the power of the Word and God's inspiring Spirit. Thus, having come to some conclusion regarding the enduring significance of a biblical passage, one must proceed to ask and answer the second question raised at the outset of our study: What, if anything, does this have to do with us and our world? (Review Chapter I on "Know the Basic Questions.")

The second question should be deliberately raised for several reasons. First, because the process of discovering what a biblical passage *means* (interpretation) and applying it to our lives (application) are two different though related processes. We do well to separate them so as to give adequate attention to what the text actually does say and mean, without rushing prematurely to applications which may be superficial or even erroneous. We do

59

well to separate them also to remind ourselves that we need not always be applying Scripture to our lives to be engaged in edifying and worthwhile Bible study. At some public and private Bible study we may devote more attention to understanding a passage, with minimal attention to present application. At other times, more energy may be devoted to discerning serious and important applications of an understood passage to contemporary life. Neither is more important than the other. They are both part of a larger process of adequate Bible study. So some need not feel extended inquiry into the text's meaning is somehow "irrelevant" or "bookish," and others need not feel that serious concern for present application of the Word is somehow "superficial" or "immature." The distortion of good Bible study as either endless inquiry into meaning or continual discussion about relevance is a disservice to all concerned and to the Word. Good Bible study involves both.

The fact that adequate Bible study must include the incarnation of that ancient Word in contemporary lives is a second reason why the application question must be deliberately raised. While much application is done rather automatically, it should not be left to chance. All Bible study at some stage must proceed to ask the enduring significance of the truth encountered and its relationship to the lives of the present readers.

The "if anything" in this question has already been considered in the preceding chapter on evaluation. It reminds us that different passages in Scripture apply to the twentieth century in different ways. Serious problems arise when passages from anywhere in the Bible are applied directly to the twentieth century without further thought.

Disillusionment is often the price for such procedures. The "if anything" does not imply that some Scripture has nothing to do with us, for all of Scripture has significance for us in one way or another — some directly, some indirectly, all with importance. This qualification reminds us that the application process begins with an understanding of where the individual passage being considered fits in the overall flow of biblical revelation and cautions against a piece-meal, proof-text sort of application.

APPLY PRINCIPLES FIRST

Just as one is well advised to interpret main points first and consider details in the light of the whole, so it is in applying the Word. It is best to identify the general principle being ennunciated and to ask regarding its significance for contemporary life. Then one may proceed to various details of the passage which may or may not apply to our day. In this way one will often perceive which features of a passage are of universal and trans-cultural significance, and which are more culturally conditioned and confined to application to a specific time and place in the past.

For example, in Matthew chapter 6 it appears that the general issue Jesus addresses is the question of authentic devotion to God—how one ought to "practice piety" (Matthew 6.1). In the process he discusses the specific examples relevant to first century Jews: giving alms (vs. 2-4), prayer in the synagogues and on the street corners (vs. 5-6), non-Jewish verbosity in prayer (vs. 7-15), and fasting (vs. 16-18). The *principle* being taught in each appears to be that true worship and all practices related to it are done sincerely to God Himself, without regard for impressing either people or God. Only this worship receives reward. Any other "worship" is in fact not worship, but an exercise done "to men" and rewarded by the fact that they observed it.

This principle applies to all cultures and all generations of believers. It does so in spite of the fact that many cultures and generations do not have synagogues, do not have the custom of public prayer on the street corners even by the pious, are not accustomed to highly repetitive and verbose prayer in pagan worship, are not familiar with religious fasting, and so on. Not only the general principle is applicable, but its application to the specific sorts of matters raised by Jesus is also valid: to practices of giving, however they are done and by whatever name they are called in different cultures, to public and private prayer, to pious practices such as fasting. Beyond this the principle would be applicable to whatever aspects of worship one might consider in whatever cultures one might name.

Sometimes this practice of applying the principle first is done almost intuitively in a sort of cultural transfer that "foreign" readers make in an attempt to transfer what they are reading into understandable equivalents in their own culture. Beyond this intuitive process, the serious student will deliberately and consistently seek to discover the central principles being set forth and will apply them first, governing application of the details of the passage by direction set by the principle. Otherwise the application of the details may even, in some instances, contradict the force of the principle. So, for instance, even if a person understood the central principle in Matthew 6.1-18 of unpretentious worship, if he or she sought to carry that out by "annointing their head" (v. 17) with oil, in North American society, the resulting coiffure would call more attention to itself than would a sad countenance. Some other cultural equivalent will have to be found to carry out the principle in this case!

BE SPECIFIC AND CONCRETE

While it is the general principles which most frequently carry across the centuries to us, those general principles must again take form in the details of our lives. Of course there is great value in clearly planting the principles themselves in our consciousness, as bases for spontaneous applications all along the way. These become points of reference in our minds which are being renewed after the image of Christ. But these principles will take on greater significance as we give consideration to specific and concrete ways in which they will be lived out for us.

Thus, if I am assured that God desires in my culture the same authentic worship described by Jesus in Matthew 6 and by many other biblical speakers elsewhere such as Malachi—unpretentious, unhypocritical, and directed solely to the King who alone is worthy of worship—I will give attention to the specific ways that will influence my worship acts and attitudes. I will ask how my worship can be less hypocritical, less pretentious, less for those around me and more for the King.

So it must be for all truth of Scripture. The student should think in terms of specific, concrete, dollars and cents, time and energy investments, of specific relationships with persons and organizations and possessions, of the real stuff out of which his or her life is made as the arena where the Word will take shape today. Significant applications will not occur in vague realms of "spirituality" or "holiness" that have nothing to do with life as it is lived.

GET STARTED WITH QUESTIONS

The ways in which the Scripture's truths intersect our lives are as varied as the myriad combinations of those truths and our complex lives. At times the Word of God convicts us of sin. At other times God speaks assurance through His Word. Sometimes our ways are condemned, sometimes confirmed. At other points we are instructed, given new information and understanding of both the past and present, and so on. If one is at a loss to know just how to start bringing the truth of a passage to the present, one may at least get underway by asking questions like the following. They are only suggestive, but can provide a starting place.

Having concluded study of a passage, one might begin by asking:

1. What sin should I confess in view of this passage?
2. What affirmations should I make in light of this Word—affirmations about God, about Christ, about myself, about others, about this world?

3. In what ways does this passage confirm good already present by God's grace in my life?
4. What changes should I make in my investment of time, money, energy, or personal resources in view of the truth of this passage?
5. What prayer should I pray for myself or my family or my friends or my enemies in light of what I have seen in the Word?

Continue the process in prayer and meditation before the Master whose Word you have studied. There is literally no end to what Jesus called "hearing and doing" His Word (Matthew 7.24).

For further study see:

Jensen. *Independent Bible Study*. pp. 61-66, 75, 153-158.
Traina. *Methodical Bible Study*. pp. 214-219.
Lincoln. *Personal Bible Study*. pp. 117-120.

Traina and Lincoln are more helpful here.

RESOURCES FOR BIBLE STUDY

Bible Study Method

Jenson, Irving L. *Independent Bible Study*. Chicago: Moody Press, 1963.

Job, John B. *How to Study the Bible*. Downers Grove, IL: Inter-Varsity Press, 1973.

Lincoln, William C. *Personal Bible Study*. Minneapolis: Bethany Fellowship, 1975.

Sterrett, T. Norton. *How to Understand Your Bible*. Downers Grove, IL: InterVarsity Press, 1974.

Traina, Robert A. *Methodical Bible Study*. Wilmore, KY: The Author, 1952.

Bible Dictionaries and Encyclopedias

Douglas, J.D. (ed.). *The New Bible Dictionary*. Grand Rapids: Eerdmans, 1962.

Tenny, Merrill C. (ed.). *Zondervan Pictorial Encyclopedia of the Bible*, 5 vols. Grand Rapids: Zondervan, 1975.

Unger, Merrill F. *Unger's Bible Dictionary*. Chicago: Moody Press, 1959.

Concordances

Strong, James. *Exhaustive Concordance of the Bible.* 1890. Reprint. Nashville: Abingdon, 1973.

Wigrim, George V. *The Englishman's Greek Concordance of the New Testament.* 1903. Reprint. Grand Rapids: Zondervan, 1976.

Wigrim, George V. *The Englishman's Hebrew and Chaldee Concordance of the Old Testament.* 1890. Reprint. Grand Rapids: Zondervan, 1972.

Young, Robert. *Analytical Concordance of the Bible.* Revised edition, 1936. Reprint. Grand Rapids: Eerdmans, n.d.

DATE DUE

F			
SEP 1 5 '86			
FEB 1 6 '88			